Employees really need to feel appreciated for the work that they do. Included in this journal are some positive things that you can say to your staff to show them that their work and their efforts are truly valued by you.

Thank you! You really did a great job
on that!

I appreciate that I never have to
check on your work – it's always
excellent!

❬◇❭

You really bring value to this
organization.

❬◇❭

You are an invaluable member of this team.

You always find a way to get
the job done - great work!

I'm really glad that your on my team.

Your work ethic is an excellent
example for everyone.

Thank you for always being willing to
go above and beyond your job.

It's clear how much pride you take in your work.

I'm impressed with how you always
get the job done on time.

Thank you for putting up with all changes going on.

I appreciate your attention to detail;
it shows through in your work.

I really appreciate your willingness to go the extra mile.

Thank you for making me look good!

I'm continually impressed by the
results that you produce!

Thank you for helping out the team
on this!

Thank you for the amazing effort you
put into that project.

You really went above and
beyond on this assignment.

You do a great job handling all the craziness around here.

_____

_____

_____

_____

_____

_____

_____

_____

_____

_____

_____

_____

_____

_____

_____

_____

_____

_____

_____

_____

*I appreciate your willingness to adapt
to changing priorities.*

Made in the USA
Columbia, SC
17 December 2019